Books in the Linkers series

Homes discovered through Art & Technology
Homes discovered through Geography
Homes discovered through History
Homes discovered through Science

Myself discovered through Art & Technology
Myself discovered through Geography
Myself discovered through History
Myself discovered through Science

Toys discovered through Art & Technology
Toys discovered through Geography
Toys discovered through History
Toys discovered through Science

Water discovered through Art & Technology
Water discovered through Geography
Water discovered through History
Water discovered through Science

First published 1996 A&C Black (Publishers) Limited
35 Bedford Row, London WC1R 4JH

ISBN 0-7136-4378-1
A CIP catalogue record for this book is available from the British Library.

Copyright © 1996 BryantMole Books

Commissioned photographs by Zul Mukhida
Design by Jean Wheeler   Picture research by Liz Harman

Consultant: Hazel Grice

Acknowledgements

Chapel Studios; 4 (right), 22 (right), Bruce Coleman; Thomas Buchholz 4 (left), Keith Gunnar 6, Guido Cozzi 7 (left), Eric Crichton 12 (right), Jane Burton 15 (left), 18 (left), C & S Hood 15 (right), Andrew J Purcell 16, 17 (right), Edward Parker; 11 (left), Positive Images; 22 (left), Science Photo Library; Dr H C Robinson 9 (left), Tony Stone; Ron Berg 11 (right), Andy Sacks 12 (left), Mike Smith 14 (left), Gay Bumgarner 17 (left), Hans Reinhard 18 (right), John Turner 19, Lori Adamski Peek 20 (left), Zefa; 3 (both), 5 and cover.

Printed and bound in Italy by L.E.G.O.

Water

discovered through
Science

Karen Bryant-Mole

Contents

Water 2

Hot and cold 4

Ice 6

Steam 8

It's waterproof 10

Plants 12

At home in sea water 14

At home in fresh
  water 16

Water as a food store 18

Staying alive 20

Clean water 22

Glossary 24

Index 24

A & C Black • London

Water

How would you describe water?

Water feels wet.
It is see-through, or transparent.

Water is a type of material.
Scientists use the word 'materials'
to mean 'what things are
made from'.
Rain is made from water.

Water is a liquid.
Liquids are materials that
can be poured.

Hot and cold

Temperature is a measure of how hot or cold something is. The temperature of water can be changed.
It can be cold, warm or hot.

Washing
We use hot water to wash our clothes and to do the washing-up.
Hot water is better at removing dirt and grease from our clothes and dishes than cold water.

Hot water

We use hot water in our baths and showers.
A hot bath or shower will warm us up on a cold day.

Cold water

Cold water can cool us down when we are hot.
Have you ever cooled down in a paddling pool on a hot day?
A drink of cold water can help us to keep cool, too.

5

Ice

When water gets very cold, it freezes. Frozen water is called ice.

Shapes

When water freezes, it changes from a liquid to a solid.
Solids can't be poured. They keep the same shape. These icicles have very sharp points.

Sliding

Large areas of frozen water usually have a smooth surface that is very slippery.
These ice skaters are having fun on the slippery ice rink.

Ice on roads is not so much fun. Cars skid very easily on ice and can cause accidents.

Melting

When the temperature of ice rises, the ice starts to melt.

Ice cubes melt in drinks as they are heated up by the warmer liquid all around them.

When snow and ice melt, the water can cause floods.

Steam

When water gets very hot it turns to steam.

Steam is a gas. Gases have no particular shape or size.

Boiling

Water changes to steam when it boils.

Have you ever watched the steam coming out of the spout of a boiling kettle? Steam is full of very tiny water droplets.

Cooking

Boiling water can be used to cook vegetables and other foods. Boiling water is extremely hot.

Never try to touch boiling water or steam.

Burns

If steam or very hot water touches skin, the skin burns.

This burn was caused by the hot water in a cup of coffee.

Burns are painful. Very bad burns can kill. You must always take care near hot water.

It's waterproof

Some materials do not let water soak into them or pass through them.
This is known as being waterproof.

Plastic
Plastic is a waterproof material. It is used to make raincoats and wellington boots.
Garden furniture is sometimes made from plastic.
Bath toys are often made from plastic, too.

Oil

Water runs off oil and wax.
Coats are sometimes made from
waxed fabric, so that rainwater runs off.
Ducks have oiled feathers.
The oil stops water soaking into
the feathers.

Skin

Our skin is waterproof, too.
So is our hair.
When we wash our bodies the water
drips back into the bath or basin.

Plants

All plants need water.

Food

Plants use sunlight and water
to make food for themselves.
With the right amount of sunlight and
water, the corn seedlings below will
grow into strong, healthy crops.
Most of our food comes from plants
or from animals that eat plants,
so water is very important to us.

Roots

Plants soak up water from the
ground through their roots.
Plants spread out their roots under
the ground, so that they can get
as much water as possible.
The water travels up the plant
to its leaves.

Dry soil

This plant is growing in soil which is too dry. It is beginning to wilt, or go floppy.

Any plant that does not get enough water will die.

At home in sea water

The salty water in the sea is a home
for many animals and plants.

Fish

Thousands of different types
of fish live in the world's seas
and oceans.
Some fish swim near
the surface.
Others live in the cold, dark
water near the sea bed.

Other animals

Lobsters, squid, shrimps and
starfish all make their homes
in the sea.
So does the seahorse in
the picture on the right.
Can you think of any other
animals that live in the sea?

Plants

Most of the plants that grow in the sea are types of seaweed. Like other plants, they need sunlight to grow.

Seaweeds are usually found quite close to the shore or near the surface of the sea.

They cannot get enough sunlight in deep water.

At home in fresh water

The water that is found in rivers, streams, lakes and ponds is called fresh water.
It is not salty, like sea water.

Fish
Different fish prefer different types of water. Some fish, like this rainbow trout, enjoy living in fast-moving river water.
Other fish, such as sticklebacks and carp, prefer the calm water of a pond.

Insects

Lots of insects live in and around ponds.

Many insects, like this dragonfly, lay their eggs just above the water. When the young hatch out, they live in the water until they become adults.

Frogs and toads

In the spring, frogs and toads lay eggs underwater. The eggs are known as frogspawn or toadspawn. Young frogs and toads live underwater. Adult frogs and toads spend most of their time on dry land.

Water as a food store

The animals that live around water often use it as a place to find food.

Animals
The animal on the right is an otter. Otters live in the banks of rivers and catch fish to eat.
Beavers and bears also hunt for fish.

Birds
These seagulls are looking for fish in the water below.
When they spot a fish, they dive down and catch it in their beak.
Other types of bird, called waders, walk around the water's edge, using their long beaks to hunt for small fish and insects.

People

People use seas
and rivers as places to
find food.

Fishermen catch fish to
sell in the fish markets.

People also eat other
sea creatures such as
crabs, shrimps, mussels
and oysters.

Staying alive

You need water to stay alive.
Almost three-quarters of your body
is made up of water.

Losing water

Every time you go to the toilet,
you lose water from your body.
You also lose water when you breathe.
When you get hot, you lose water
through your skin, as sweat.
This man is sweating after a long run.

Drinks

The water that you lose has
to be replaced.
Drinks replace most of the water.
Squash, juice, milk and fizzy drinks
all contain water.

Food

There is water in many foods, too.
Cucumbers, strawberries, celery and oranges
are all mostly made of water.
Any food that is juicy probably contains
a lot of water.

Clean water

Bodies

We need to wash our bodies to stop them getting dirty and smelly.
We can pick up germs from things we touch.
It is a good idea to wash your hands after you have been to the toilet and before you eat.

Clothes

We also need clean water to wash our clothes.
If we did not wash them, they, too, would become dirty and smelly.

Drinking water
The water that we drink must be clean.

Dirty water can cause diseases. The water that comes out of our taps has been cleaned at a water treatment works and then piped to our homes.

Water is the most important material in the world. Without it, there would be no life on Earth.

Glossary

crops food plants that are grown by farmers
diseases illnesses
replaced put back
sea bed the ground under the sea

seedlings young plants grown from seeds
shore land at the edge of a sea
surface the top side of something

Index

animals 14, 18

birds 18
burns 9

clean water 22–23
cold water 5
cooking 9

drinks 5, 20

fish 14, 16, 19
food 12, 18–19, 21
fresh water 16–17
frogs 17

hot water 4, 5, 8, 9

ice 6–7
ice cubes 7
icicles 6
insects 17

materials 3, 10
melting 7

oil 11

people 19, 20–21, 22–23
plants 12–13, 15
plastic 10

roots 12

sea water 14–15
seaweeds 15
skating 7
skin 11
steam 8–9
sunlight 12, 15

temperature 4–5
toads 17

washing 4, 22
waterproof 10–11

How to use this book

Each book in this series takes a familiar topic or theme and focuses on one area of the curriculum: science, art and technology, geography or history. The books are intended as starting points, illustrating some of the many different angles from which a topic can be studied. They should act as springboards for further investigation, activity or information seeking.

The following list of books may prove useful.

Further books to read

Series	Title	Author	Publisher
	Simple Science	A. Wilkes	Usborne
First Nature	Fishes	A. Wheeler	Usborne
Jump! Science	Experiment with Water	B. Murphy	Watts
Lift Off!	Fish	J. Richardson	Watts
Science Activities	Science with Water	K. Woodward	Usborne
See for Yourself	Snow and Ice	Davies & Oldfield	A&C Black
	Rain		
Starting Science	Water	Davies & Oldfield	Wayland
Stopwatch	Dragonfly	Barrie Watts	A&C Black
	Newt		
	Stickleback		
	Tadpole and Frog		
Talkabout	Water	Henry Pluckrose	Watts
Threads	Water	B. Walpole	A&C Black